GEMMA JACKSON
Aprire

BROKEN SLEEP BOOKS

Published 2020,
Broken Sleep Books:
Cornwall / Wales

brokensleepbooks.com

First Edition

Lay out your unrest.

Publisher/Editor: Aaron Kent
Editor: Charlie Baylis

Typeset in UK by Aaron Kent

Broken Sleep Books is committed to
a sustainable future for our planet,
and therefore uses print on
demand publication.

brokensleepbooks@gmail.com

ISBN: 978-1-913642-05-1

Aprire

Gemma Jackson

Contents

heard once about a man
                    cut him

self open to
sag jaws [they]
            say this: you are 2 moons full

&

it's just a phase
bookwalled-like and tongued touch where the sou
nd was meant to go breathing witness shaped bodyslates
exhale.

        unassimilated intrusions are the sexy kind muted
stirrings fluidly/so fluidy/so.much.fluid. wet enough for mama-pecks
                        & clean sides in case [they] ask
                            something she might grow into.

you don't have to say it that way/do you/say it/that/way of saying
collarbones are for chumps anyway of saying is this expressive/wide
enough staged in cardboard angles last seen pouring herself through the
cracks in [their] back teeth a phantasmatic tracing told [them]:

first, she crawled.

stuffing the mouth, next, was a purely aesthetic study
those bee-sting globs only palatable with speed
& you there
fisting gums. all knuckle-pulp
& echoes

in the gentler version there are sister-shaped cotton lungs
& she calls it a verb and bullshit.

now this thing that you rest your wrists on is pink and squishy
maybe there's something in that too
grief ritualised
with this need to always be attached asking
what colour do you need to serve femme realness
to occupy space

sick of awareness. afflicting your own by eating breakfast for lunch
again to fuck up the space time continuum after correcting your tendency
to put mums where they don't belong.

turned to astrology as a last result for these ebbs and flows. it told you the
stars gave you a profound need for lists.

found a medusa on the table that was too big for pockets.

ate day long fruit all day for softer insides.

asked what it required. [they] replied "what".

made a general gesture of writing down the significance of that.

screamed her head into the world.

at what point do we address the   room?

feels more honest to hold her in paint.

rejecting displays of unresolved somethings.

[they] express in our stomachs now.

in jasmine corners, always swallowing.

this is meant to be hopeful in a way, with the right standpoint.

told her you squeezed it right out
without making this a strip tease
except the clothes are wet
and there aren't any clothes
because we're naked and crying.

is this your way
of forcing her into representation
lined transpersonal: a consequence
of expressive limits and ambiguous bone structures
left cheek leaning more in your favour

write a muscle right out like that
let them think you've been chewing that biro, god
you are always chewing that biro like
no one told you

bred habitually sexed-up-like
of course clomping involves sideways dips and canines
more stringy choreography: imagine colour
tacked in the gaps you made

this was never a conversation
for the woman who gave you pages
from spotty signal
and pretend lingua-deafness.

enter fleshy
  rooms realistic enough
   for painting
         nude voices
          an entire veil, edible and hoarse
   prophetic.
 advised to use prominences
 skimming walls of noses,
             names,
      excessiveness.
took notes on the one hand
defiled by eating pretty, if it counts
a waistband
in a chapter written on
what else other than reflex than breathing extremities
                  wipe feet here.
                a distance away, imagining toughness.
                to recount the shape of a word:
                        nip it quick and slow
                        a shredded utter
with the mask turned inwards to a human creature, seeping
they did half the rushing, creating a visual
but it's dense and chews like cardboard
sounded for sitting,
post-roots/post-return.

you're running on a bit now
in letter shape fingers
                    hammered.

there's a start here
felt it pricked
went for it in the back seat
romantic, like.

god. oh god. go od.d.d. oh.
wanted fi-sure, oh.
kept meaning to ask if
lasers were involved
felt only pressed absence
                    neat.

smear me
like your smart screen.
like you're losing air.

and it's tucked away
in my gullet.
something about awareness

of jaws
their propensity to expand
muscular only in aches
duck face fallacies
disrupting

wiry figurines
stacking sleeping motions
in pottery stillness

nestling human ridges
between chemical peels and
bus tickets just out
of eye sight.

I know now. what happens when they give you language.
start sleeping sideways. wake up in bunches.
that shirt was oversized for a reason. perching on woodchips.
nailbeds grey, or they smell like they should be.
an old solution. but it's rhythmic.
and your body likes the inside sounds.
wispy. a word I never gave you.
something you'd expect. guessed my incense.
that I burned at all.

it got embedded once. crackled at the pressure.
the morning was blue. told you what happens on rooftops.
between inhales on tiptoes. how we rationalize forward.
how it's awkward to tilt. how blisters are afterthoughts of big
ideas.
you stayed, half-drawn and I nearly bleached my hair.

there's a train for this. I'm wearing that winter coat on it.
pressing the button like bruises. is it reasonable?
to empty you in cafés. when no one ever asks to sit in that.

an expectation, peeled back. that you'd taste the same.
was it borrowed? in the end. remembered in song-skips.
and you: counting Verona footsteps.
the map was plastic: what I remember. imagined you
in greenish air, holding your breath. the next number
emptied into it. a dead sound.

a note a day. in memory of that grey strand you tried to find.
because it was always literal. in lines is definition. yanked tight.
millimetres in wrapped palms. repeating wont with forgotten
punctuation
and open Os. there is so much that I understand about yellow.
spilt innocuous behind my eyelids. still blinking.

got ok with the pressable parts. with the fur that wove chin tucks
girlish but still too full.
got ok with the solidness of walls. with the tables too
that mix of cement and wood, painted not-white needed to grow
up and how many women does it take to wear down
that leg.

your mind works
 .our mind works
in that way
you mind shadows
& low-res suffering

        it needs to hang
in an interesting way
but first it needs
to be

written typed
biological breath
points & pockets
understanding that

to cut is
   to be
plosive &
     breath
less &
squared. away but
absent of. gaps found in
connectors. grasping out. alphabetical

give it a page.
give it miles & miles.
you cannot navigate shapes

without space
we are without
where we insist
we sit right in
without middles

& someone will read you
back to back

they will want a separation
of you

                          a mirror, a girl &
                          she had 3 to choose from

as you pick at excess
    in EDM patterns

                          mouthing vulva
                          & that swiss army knife, dug up
                              popping eyes. inscribed

juddery voice, whirling in acid
ic-- heaves.

                          a phrase, thrown to disturb

graduated pain
so you read essays &

                    later caught with corduroy, pitched between knees
                              handwash for the visceral
            chi trova un amico, trova un tesoro, two years from now

mitigate what you know:

                          an alt-opus. you never danced
                          contemporary, but once you flooded a cinema
                              & flew tears.

& yet you
stick needles
a stomach full
& say it's out of love

        & we will skip over canals
        leapfrogging bowed steps
        it's bad luck, otherwise
        kissing on the watery edge of tails

I needed a cord
to unwind
to close my eyes
let the brickwork sand down the callouses
yeah, those ones.

        can only mumble on suitcases
        how they will be bursting with baked-beans
        as I shake my wrist at posters that bloomed
        behind a sofa, in faux-leather
        bit saucy

        if you were a jigsaw piece
        you'd be the sky
        don't ask me if you're the corner
        that requires the rest &
        eye contact,
        you see.

now we are climbing through windows

with liquid muscles & teetering

flickering desktops

singeing eye-liner tips

dripping chin length

a single point & it is a stream.

they keep asking you for a different tongue

& you bite it to double-check

& all there is, is blood

& it's the same colour

& still, they will ask.

something has moved. you feel it

the windowsill caught your tights the same as always

before the scream was swallowed by letterless prayers

& the urge to run a finger down a wing

intersecting a false grief

it wasn't born here

but that balcony edge is where she died.

they are hungry boys
uttering pleas
for words on platters
on low sofas
toes snaked under shins
a bathroom full of house-plants
refracted murky as you search for the tissue
& blot at coffee stains collected in lip crevices
urging sound with little sense for shapes
it bubbles up. infuses with the camomile tea, balancing
on a knee cap. what will it take?
to speak a mind with strategic structures, fluidly
existing in the transitions of these requests. that is to say
they come only after you.

ma, ti senti aperta? ti senti matta?
she is searching for your
equilibrium & you
are sure it has melted down
into the hair baby-like littering your chest
broad you, little succubus of courage
-an absorber.

how could you possibly
expect to be lead
confes//

               //sing in erased poetics
to stutter exits & moralise
& then,

they echo.

the problem
is that you are
aware. & you fear
musicality that condenses
trivial, really to rhyme organs
that have a tendency to yelp like Morrissey

same font
buried in rucksacks
we won't tell him how
only that Top Gun's involved
& you endured box-hair-colour smell
to bundle a flight suit. a close, set to the 80s

moonlit
mothering typ
ings, unchecked
but strong-armed by your
benching to fever-drums & coordination
of thoughts: we're not even trying now, are we?

try saying
funky, unironically
set intentions. listlessly
it's a whole vibe & what's a
mesh-body, time-lapsing all over this
god damn kids. god damn kids & their new age

baby.
he wants
to be a bunny,
baby. like you left them
believing as you conceived
bullet-to-do's. in café's, with the wrong change

she is
writhing &
the shapes in
your hair are the reason
why it took the cheekbones you used
to write poetry on. fingernails in wood. dig.

you are
all caught up
in blasé patterns. figure
that they'll know. one blink
that print is porous/crooked in the right
light. she'd missed your smell, she said. soft.

dazzle me.
what I think
when I think of
loving, it is black &
white & fairylit & full of
squared bookcases & your toes, peeping

some you
will not tell
how long it took
to wrap Patti around
how she is quilty. how she
elbows out space in your lines with horses

there is
a binding
it presses. colours
swelling on eye-lids
it has a name but that is
kinda heavy, considering. don't you think?

chant it
you only
inhaled it to
breathe anyway.
a pleasurable pause
tapping feet on platforms. a mind/a mouth.

Acknowledgements

Some of these poems have previously appeared in
DATABLEED 10, edited by Nell Perry & Juha Virtanen.
Dorothy Lehane, countless thank yous for your continual
support and for pushing me to get my work out there. First
book down! Nathan Hassall, I'll never remember how to
spell your last name, but I will always be your biggest fan.
Liv Watts & Zoë Da Poian, this book's base rests on that day
that you rescued me in a taxi in Valencia & I will forever be
grateful for you both. Giuliana Salmaso, this is a book on
female strength & you are the strongest woman I know. I
am endlessly inspired by you. Last but never least, Caterina
Birolo. You have played so many important roles in my life
in such a short space of time, all of them unexpected; all of
them poetry.

LAY OUT YOUR UNREST

www.ingramcontent.com/pod-product-compliance
Lightning Source LLC
Chambersburg PA
CBHW071942020426
42331CB00010B/2975